AN AMERICAN BESTIARY
By Eugene J. McCarthy

Illustrated by Christopher Millis

Lone Oak Press

To Kaye

EJ McCarthy

An American Bestiary
By Eugene J. McCarthy

Illustrated by Christopher Millis

ISBN 1-883477-33-6
Library of Congress CIP 99-068856

Published by
Lone Oak Press

Contents

AAA

THE HIGH-LEVEL ADVISOR

High-Level Advisors are closely related to park pigeons. Both have a migratory instinct; they also have a homing instinct. They bow and coo a lot. They strut and waddle. They tilt their iridescent heads whenever a President speaks. They are by nature freeloaders. They move to and from the White House and other Executive office buildings. Sometimes they are driven out because of election results or because they have fallen into disfavor with a President, or with one of his principal aides. But usually after a decent waiting period they return to serve either the same President who sent them packing or one of his successors. Some, driven from the White House, find refuge in academic cloisters. Some roost on the capitals of columns of well-established foundations, supported by money made in steel, oil, or automobiles. Others find a temporary home in established law firms, from which they sometimes make quick flights back to government agencies and financial institutions. Democrats tend to migrate during the off season to the Brookings Institution, Republicans to the American Enterprise Institute. These havens are like the Canadian marshes maintained by Ducks Unlimited - havens of breeding, incubation, and rest, where the High-Level Advisors can flock to strut, to waddle, and to wait.

The Viable Alternative

Distinguishing between the Viable and the Non-Viable Alternative is a formidable challenge even for experts. It is comparable to the test of distinguishing between the poisonous and non-poisonous mushroom. (Although failure to distinguish properly between the Viable and Non-Viable Alternative does not have consequences of such immediate, evident, and absolute seriousness as does failure to distinguish properly between the poisonous and the non-poisonous mushroom.)

Non-Viable Alternatives, as a rule, are not difficult to find. They usually hang around, hoping to be noticed. They sit with arms folded and will not be budged. They tend to be stumbled over. Stumbling over a Non-Viable Alternative can result in great loss of time and may leave the Alternative hunter without a real Alternative.

Many Viable Alternatives are short-lived. An Alternative that is Viable one day may be dead the next day. On the other hand, a change in climate, especially political climate, may cause the revitalization of a dead or torpid Alternative. Some Alternatives have been known to revive after living in a state of suspended animation for years.

Little need be said of a third variety, the Unthinkable Alternative. The best that can be claimed for Unthinkable Alternatives is that they are regularly, but regretfully, thought about.

Alternative experts are distinguished by their language. Like lawyers and foreign policy experts, they say things such as "yes but" or "either/or" and "on the one hand and then on the other." When "Either/or" Alternatives meet, only one can survive. "Both/and" Alternatives, on the other hand, can live together - if not in harmony, at least within the tolerable range of adjustment.

Viable Alternatives, if not recognized and noticed, will often lie around making reproachful sounds and saying something that sounds like "I told you so."

THE ANTELOPE SITUATION

Senator Millikin of Colorado was noted for his being the first and most certain and most accurate member of the Senate in identifying what he called "the antelope situation." Millikin represented Colorado, a state which has many antelope. Antelope observers and hunters note that there is a moment at which antelope which seem to be grazing quietly, confident that they are unobserved, will suddenly raise the white flag of their tails, and speed away, over a rise and into the security of a gully or a ravine or a draw.

Millikin could sense when a comparable condition had arrived in Senate deliberations, when that body was about to panic and vote without reason or at least without good reason, usually on proposals to reform the Congress, reorganize it, establish codes of behavior, and the like. When he sensed that the moment of flight was about to arrive the Senator would say, "The antelope time has come. There is nothing for us to do but paint a white strip on the seat of our pants, panic, and vote, with the unity of a herd of antelope taking flight."

THE AURA

The Aura was noted first in high places, marked by mystery (an Aura of mystery or a mysterious aura), and associated with the divinities. Later the Aura moved down to the range of heroes. Warriors began to show up with Auras of invincibility. So the Auras descended gradually from high places to the fields of battle, to the realms of religion and politics. Leaders in all of these fields sought Auras.

The Aura did not rest with these relatively lofty callings, but descended even farther. It became domesticated. New varieties of Auras showed up. The Aura of domesticity became common along with the Proletarian Aura and the Aura of the Common Man. When the common man made a mistake, it became known as Human Aura.

Television commentators are unusually keen observers of Auras. They can see an Aura coming from afar and can identify it quickly, in much the same way that they can spot a Momentum gathering, even in fog or rain.

Despite decline from the near-supernatural to the natural, from the ceremonial to the practical, Auras generally remain proud and of good spirit. Like the goat they remember their beginnings and hold their heads high.

BBB

Beagle Brains

Employees in government agencies (the same may be true of employees of large corporations, by nature, by choice, or by a conditioning process) are likely to take on the character of the Beagle or of Beagles.

It is in the nature of every Beagle, other things being equal, to look more or slightly less, like every other Beagle and to act like every other Beagle. This is the nature of Beagles, a result of their breeding, which explains why any hope that a Beagle may sometime be chosen as best breed at Westminster is a futile hope.

It is folly (for a Beagle) to think of being the best of breed because ideally the best Beagle is the Beagle that is most like every other Beagle. Not better or worse, not more intelligent or more stupid. A Beagle that is singular, in some way outstanding, violates the basic principle and essence of Beagles.

A better Beagle might lose interest in rabbits, be indifferent, or attracted to other animal scents and sights say foxes, raccoons, deer, even bear. The best Beagle is the one that comes closest to being an average Beagle. Therefore like foreign service officers, the average Beagle is the best Beagle.

Beagles do vary slightly in size and in color but the real uniformity is of mind and spirit as physically found in brain structure. Which explains why the N.I.H., and other institutions into brain study, use Beagle brains as their standard, since every Beagle Brain is essentially like every other Beagle Brain.

In their higher faculties of mind Beagles are in many respects like a lower order of angels. All and each are of one mind and purpose. Experts on angels say that all angels in one choir are like all other angels in that choir. Every Cherubim therefore is like every other Cherubim. They have at all times the same thoughts. They have the same desires and purposes. So, too, every Seraphim is like every other member of that choir.

A Beagle that is different, singular, or "better" would be marked and subject to being cast out or down as Lucifer was when he attempted to be different.

The Beagle dimension was demonstrated in recent State Department dealings with Sadaam Hussein on the matter of Kuwait.

April Glaspie reported that the State Department did not think Sadaam was so stupid as to believe that when the Department indicated Kuwait was his problem that he would believe it.

This is the kind of problem one might encounter in dealing with Beagles.

President Johnson liked Beagles. He kept two of them at the White House and said that (like some Senators) they liked to be picked up by their ears.

THE BOLL-WEEVILS

Boll-weevils is the name that has been given by the press and by liberal democrats, or even, regular democrats, some from the south, to Southern Democrats, who run as Democrats, but who after elected, regularly vote Republican but do not formally defect in the manner of Senator Thurmond of South Carolina and Senator Gramm who formally became Republicans.

HAIR & HIDE BRANDS

The Johnson Administration reflected the Texas and cattle handling of the President, in action and in language, even in metaphor.

The President was known as being very possessive, ready to use the pronoun "my" rather freely, and without distinction, as in my party, my congress, my vice-president, my ranch, my cows, my helicopters, etc.

The LBL brand was strongly in evidence. Those threatened by were distinguished as hair brands and as hide brands. A hair-brand is temporary, imposed by simply cutting the brand letters, or forms into the hair or burning it lightly so as to singe hair and not hide. It is a temporary brand which disappears when the hair grows out. A hide brand goes deeper. It is permanent, burned into the hide of the branded animal. Critics of President Johnson's possessiveness were heard to say that the barbecues on the LBJ ranch did not always start out to be barbecues, but sometimes were branding parties that got out of control.

TIGHT & OTHER BUDGETS

Budgets, grown more or less in the dark and fed with special nutrients, inflation additives, cost-plus vitamins, and normal accretions, rise from the murky waters of public finance in various forms. They are regularly identified by those who present them as lean and sober, generally as tight, sometimes as frugal and austere, often as bare-boned. They usually are seen by others as padded, bloated, and larded with fat.

Budgets may appear impregnable, but they live a perilous life. In the familiar life cycle, a Budget no sooner appears than cries are heard to "cut the Budget!" One then observes the cut across the board, the trimming away of fat, and the cut that goes to the bone.

Tight Budgets are believed to suffer distress. Politicians, always sensitive to the discomfort of animals and the displeasure of the Humane Society, are especially sensitive to the discomfort of the Budget. Given half a chance, they will attempt to treat its discomfort with bromides, skin relaxers, sitz baths, and upward revisions of the revenue estimates.

Tight Budgets, with assistance, have been known to shed their skins as snakes do, or as some crabs shed their shells, thus relieving the pressure and making what appeared to be a tight Budget a pleasantly loose one.

THE BUG UNDER THE CHIP

"There is a bug under the chip" is an expression used by Texans and other politicians from Western Cattle raising states. Its exact meaning is subject to disagreement and different interpretations. Factually, it simply describes the experience of turning over a buffalo chip or a dry or drying deposit of cow manure and finding busy at work an insect known as the dung beetle.

This discovery seems to be surprising to some observers, and a slightly shocking experience. Actually, it should be accepted and recognized as a desirable reality. The function of the dung beetle is to break and disperse concentrations of cow manure. This it does by making balls of the basic material and rolling them some distance from the concentrated mass. Then it digs a hole, deposits the ball of manure in the hole, and lays an egg on the deposit. When the egg hatches the larva feeds on the manure, becomes an adult insect and carries on its instinctive functions. Its work accomplishes two good purposes; it spreads fertilizer and breaks up concentrations of the same, which if not dispersed either kills grass or encourages a growth that cattle will not eat.

Australia had serious problems when cattle were introduced into that country; problems solved by the introduction of dung beetles from Africa. A bug under the chip is cause for rejoicing in Australia.

THE BLOATED BUREAUCRACY

Among the most familiar creatures of the political seas is the bloated Bureaucracy. The species is almost always accompanied by its adjective. Mill in 1848 wrote of the Dominant Bureaucracy. A decade later, according to the OED, an unidentified writer spoke of the Brigand Bureaucracy of China. In our own time, we encounter the Entrenched Bureaucracy. But the preferred form, used by cultivated orators and writers everywhere, is Bloated Bureaucracy.

Bloat is no laughing matter; a bloated government has serious digestive problems. The more it eats, the more it wants; the more it wants, the more it eats.

The BB has a life span that ranges somewhere between the infinite and the eternal. This partly owing to the languid nature of the species: the Bloated Bureaucracy cannot be hurried; it swims at its own pace. The BB's longevity also is attributed to the thick scales with which its body is armored. Through this protective covering the barbed shaft can seldom penetrate. Editors, Senators, taxpayers, Jimmy Carter - they have all had a crack at insulting the Bloated Bureaucracy. Nothing takes. The fossil remains of this durable creature have been carbon-dated from the tombs of the pharaohs and may be encountered in Washington and in the several state capitols to this very day.

CCC

CUTTING CATTLE

It is very difficult to get one cow or steer to leave a herd. However, a few critters may be separated without too much trouble. Once corralled, the one wanted can be kept in the pen while the others are released to rejoin the herd. This technique was applied by President Johnson in 1964 when he feared that Senator Kennedy might make a move to secure the vice-presidential nomination. Robert Kennedy at the time was Attorney General in the Johnson cabinet. The President did not announce that he would not choose the Attorney General, but that he would not pick any one who was in the cabinet.

THE CHAMELEON

Many politicians have been compared to the chameleon, their problem

best described by Carl Sandburg who wrote:
"Remember the chameleon. He was a well-behaved chameleon and nothing could be brought against record. As a chameleon he had done the things that should have been done, and left undone the things that should have been left undone. He was a first-class, unimpeachable chameleon and nobody had anything on him. But he came to a Scotch plaid and tried to cross it. In order to cross he had to imitate six different yarn colors, first one, then another, and then back to the first or second. He was a brave chameleon and died at the crossroads, true to his chameleon instincts."

Nelson Rockefeller had trouble of this kind in the 1960 campaign. 'There were three Republican strands. The most advanced group who said there were problems and something should be done about them, but not now. There was another strand who said there were problems and that we should do less about them than we were doing or attempting to do. A third group simply said there were no problems. Rockefeller got along with all three definable groups, until he said there were problems and something should be done about them - now.

That was too much. Rockefeller attempted to cross the Scotch plaid.

THE CHARISMA

The Charisma is closely related to the Aura, although it differs in several respects. The range of the Aura is wider than that of the Charisma. The Aura is less likely to attach itself to particular persons, although it sometimes does. More commonly it associates itself with larger movements of history, with events, or with group actions. The Charisma, however, is highly personal, like the one-person dog.

Until recently the Charisma attached itself only to persons of strong religious or mystical inclination. For some reason, possibly the decline of religion and mysticism and the rise of secularism, Charismas have become less discriminating. They have become secularized and identified with purposes far less elevated than their original commitments - or identified with no purposes at all.

Charismas can be cultivated - that is, raised in captivity. But the more common way to obtain one is to capture it in the wild (it most often is found among Charismas trees) and then to domesticate it.

Even a Charisma raised in captivity carries a strain of restlessness. If not properly nurtured and cared for it may revert to its natural state and leave the person to whom it was attached, much like the falcon.

When a Charisma vanishes, it leaves its owner destitute and at a loss to explain what has happened to his former powers. With Charisma in attendance, one can make mistakes of judgment without being challenged, commit immoral acts without being criticized, and generally act with freedom and panache. A person with the right Charisma can do almost anything.

CHICKENS

Several years ago the University of Virginia Technical School released a report which shed light (or denied light) which helped explain the behavior of chickens and also applied to the conduct of some politicians.

The Virginia science professor concluded that if red and yellow light wavelengths could be kept from passing through the eyes of chickens or reaching the hypothalamus it would not be triggered to send a message to the pituitary glands to release hormones to begin the reproductive cycle. The scientist concluded that if the red and yellow wavelengths could be kept from passing through the eyes of the chickens the reproductive urges would be controlled, reduced in strength, or eliminated altogether, and that the birds, both male and female would be more docile and less agitated. Contented hens would lay more eggs, and both male and females, undisturbed by sexual drives would eat quietly, use feed more efficiently; that cocks would spend less time fighting, and the tendency of chickens to peck each other to death might be moderated.

This report gave scientific support to a chicken handling process used by Minnesota farmers fifty years ago. A serious problem in handling chickens arose then especially during the winter months when because of zero and sub-zero weather it was necessary to keep the chickens in relatively small coops. Crowded conditions seemed to move chickens to picking each other, sometimes even unto death.

Farmers did the best they could. They thought about the problem and concluded that it was the blood on a chicken, accidentally wounded which attracted the attacks. They reasoned that if chickens could not see the blood on the wounded bird, they would not peck or pick on it. The next step was to find a way of concealing the blood from the cannibalistic flock. The farmers concluded that the thing to do was to paint the windows of the chicken coop red or rose colored, or to install rose-colored glass and put in rose tinted light bulbs.

The procedure seemed to work despite the word of scientists of the time that chickens were color-blind. The procedure seemed to work despite the unsoundness of the theory. What was done for the wrong scientific reason accomplished what the modern scientist believes can be accomplished by fitting chickens with contact lenses (or glasses) which will screen out the disturbing light rays. The findings may have some bearing on the judgment passed on one Minnesota politician of that early period, namely, "that if he were a chicken he would have been able to see which member of the flock was bleeding even behind the red or rose-tinted windows or in the muted glow of a pink light bulb."

The behavior of politicians fitted with the chicken scientist's lenses would be a real test of his theory.

THE COCKEREL STEP

The early stages of the Carter Presidency were marked by the "cockerel step" which the Welsh poet wrote of as the step by which the light shortened the sleep of earth and night. It is the step that marks the young, insecure rooster as distinguished from that of the established cock of the walk, or of the yard. It is marked by three separable and definable stages. In the first stage the rooster raises on foot, holding the leg close to his body, suggesting great restraint and growing tension. During this stage the young rooster looks thoughtful and confident. In the second stage, the tension is released, the foot is thrust forward positively and aggressively and then brought to a stop, well above the ground. In the third stage the leg is retracted, the claws relaxed. The foot is drawn back slowly and placed on the ground at just about the same spot at which the first stage of the step began. If the first step was taken with the right leg, the second, similar in all respects, will follow with the left.

Thus in the campaign and after, Mr. Carter denounced the Internal Revenue Code as a disgrace to the human race. The foot had been lifted from the ground. Then he proposed radical if not violent changes. The loopholes would be closed, interest paid on home mortgages would no longer be allowed as a deduction, the valleys of the code would be raised, and the hills and mountains lowered, the income tax code would be made straight as the way of the Lord.

But hold a moment. The extended leg hold, suspended like the blade of the guillotine. Slowly it is retracted. The claw relaxed. How about settling for an increase in the investment credit, and a tax rebate of $0 dollars. But hold again. No so fast or so far. Let us consider again both the rebate and the investment credit. Down comes the foot in the same scratch mark.

Then the other foot comes up. Agencies will be abolished, inflation controlled by drastic means. Then the hold and the retracted and decently put down a little behind the spot from which it was lifted.

The Clinton Administration is showing similar signs of progress.

THE COLUMNIST:

There is no safe way of dealing with columnists.

The best policy for office holders is to evade their attention, never seek their approval, and ignore their criticism.

They are dangerous in the way of Bonasus, or Bonnacon, described in the Medieval Bestiary as:

An animal born in Asia, which has a bullish head,
and from then on the rest of his body like a horse's mane.

The horns are curled round upon themselves
with such a multiple convolution

That if anybody bumps against them
he does not get hurt.

But however much its front end
does not defend this monster.

Its belly end is amply sufficient.

For when it turns to run away
it emits a fart with the contents

Of its large intestine
which covers three acres.

And any tree that it reaches
catches fire.

Thus he drives away his pursuers.

The Consensus

The Consensus is a problem to the natural scientists. It has no before. It has no after. It is a coming together not unlike the aardvark, which did not evolve from any other animal and is not evolving into any other. It follows that it is no easy job to generate a Consensus.

The Consensus also is like the Mandate. It can be compared to a Gathering Momentum that has not yet started to move. It has some of the attributes of the Aura. But no one of these - the Mandate, the Momentum, or the Aura - can fairly be said to be like a Consensus.

The Consensus is especially noted for its digestive system. It chews a cud and has three stomachs, but it eats only soft food because it lacks a gizzard to handle hard facts. The Consensus has little structure and very few bones. Generally it is said of a Consensus only that it appears to be. Hence when it disintegrates it vanishes quite completely, leaving behind only a fine powder, or ash, which does not lend itself readily to postmortem (or to psychoanalysis either).

The Broad-Based Constituency

A cow never voluntarily sits down. Because it has several stomachs, when it lies down it does so first with its front half and then with its rear half. The Broad-Based Constituency, on the contrary, never voluntarily stands up. Its strength and appeal lie in its broad base. Its movement consists principally in a slow pivot on its nether quarters.

Politicians constantly make the mistake of seeking Broad-Based Constituencies. The thought is that a BBC is reasonably stable and not likely to wander off, as narrow-based or narrow-hipped Constituencies often do. In time, however, Broad-Based Constituencies become a burden on their owners. As they become broader and broader their mobility decreases until in some cases they cannot move, even in search of food. They have to be fed incessantly.

Possessors of Broad-Based Constituencies frequently develop nervous habits. They worry whether the Constituency is happy, whether it needs water, or more food, or just reassurance. Often they will leave in the middle of a party just to run home and give the constituency a few biscuits and kibbles and a glass of cold milk.

In consequence of its sedentary existence, the Broad-Based Constituency suffers from nerve and muscle deterioration in its lower back and demands to be regularly stroked or massaged. BBCs also become calloused and insensitive in their basic areas, developing an ailment comparable to bargeman's bottom, which is in turn comparable to housemaid's knee or barfly's elbow. It is very painful - so painful that it sometimes drives a Broad-Based Constituency to overcome its inertia and move, leaving the politician who has nurtured it bereft.

THE COWBIRD TECHNIQUE

The cowbird lays its eggs in other birds nests, letting the host bird hatch the egg and nourish the newborn birds until they fly away. The cowbird then accepts the hatched and nourished birds as one of its own; as applied to politicians, it designates one who introduces an issue or a program, allows others to develop the issue and program, and then takes credit for what is produced.

A process not altogether different from that of speech writers who implant ideas in speeches of their principals, and then, if the idea is successful, go public, claiming it as their own, in the manner of surrogate mothers or fathers, if the child turns out to be special.

THE MOUNTING CRISIS

It might be supposed, considering the nature of the beasts, that Crises are as rare as pileated woodpeckers. This was true in another era, but in our own century Crises have returned from the brink of extinction. Now Crises abound. In 1978 alone, merely in the city of Washington, scores of Crises were sighted and recorded. Taking the first quarter as typical, one recalls that Mr. Carter was grappling with the Coal Crisis, the Dollar Crisis, the Mideast Crisis, the Energy Crisis, and a Crisis of Confidence - all at the same time. The President also was attempting to cope with a Crisis on the farms, a Crisis in the cities, and a Crisis in his relations with blacks, Congress, and the Jewish voters of Florida and New York. A Crisis was approaching, or so it was said, in his own political fortunes.

The Mounting Crisis is the most familiar form. At some point in its life span, every Crisis mounts. Experts are divided on the question of what becomes of the Mounting Crisis. Some authorities believe that Crises are resolved; some report that Crises fade. From our own observations we have concluded that Crises simply disappear. Sometimes they also reappear. One day they are all over page one; they dominate the evening news on TV. The next day one detects no mention of them. Then, after some lapse of time, they return, still mounting. A Sturdy Crisis, fed a balanced diet of facts and rumors, can keep this up indefinitely. Consider Mideast Crisis. It has been mounting for four millennia.

CUT & RUN

"Cut and run" is a phrase applied to those cattle, usually only one or a few, that break out of a herd drive. Sometimes applied to infantry soldiers who break out of an advancing unit in the face of fire, or to politicians who break party ranks, rather than be stampeded. The phrase was applied by President Johnson and other advocates and supporters of the Vietnam War to those who would not support the war.

DDD

THE STAGGERING DEFICIT

It is sometimes thought that nothing new ever emerges among the fish, fowl, and mammals that comprise a political Bestiary. But new species do come along now and then. One of the more interesting is the Deficit.

We have chosen to illustrate the Staggering Deficit, the breed most commonly found in the conservative press of the southeastern states. The Macon (Ga.) News, indeed, has never been known to record any variety but the Staggering Deficit. This is also true of the Charleston News and Courier, the Greensboro News, and the Richmond News Leader.

Yet it is one of the curious properties of this remarkable beast that the same Deficit known as a Staggering Deficit in Columbia, Savannah, and Jacksonville is known as the Not Intolerable Deficit in Los Angeles, New York, and Boston. One finds the Stimulative Deficit in The New York Times, the Modest Deficit in the New Republic, and the Acceptable Deficit in the Washington Post. These are all the same Deficits. Astounding!

From 1866 through 1893, no Deficits whatever were recorded. Some optimistic fellows thought Deficits had become extinct. Then Deficits began to be sighted again, and except for ten years of oblivion during the administrations of Harding, Coolidge, and Hoover, Deficits have been around every since.

The Staggering Deficit came to prominence in the period after World War II, notably in the budgets of 1953 and 1959. After a memorably horrendous appearance in 1968, the Staggering Deficit became the Recurring Deficit. All Deficits have been classified as Recurring since 1970. It is expected that this condition will continue.

DEMOCRATS & THE PREHISTORIC PIGS

In contrast with the Republicans, Democrats of recent years or decades have not been well represented by the donkey whose credentials were never very well established and might better have chosen as their animal representative the five prehistoric pigs (now historic) that were found in a perfect circle. The explanation is that since pigs perspire through their mouths and noses, their noses become very cold as the temperature drops below freezing, and these pigs as the ice age came on, in order to keep their noses warm, formed the perfect circle and froze to death with slightly warm noses.

THE CREDIBLE DETERRENT

The Deterrent does not fit easily into any category of beasts. It is not a working animal. It is not a hunter, a watchdog, a guardian, or a defender. The theory behind its breeding runs counter to the traditionally accepted assertion that "the best defense is a strong offense." The principle bred into the Deterrent is that the best defense is a strong counterattack. The Deterrent does not know, or particularly care to know, what is coming. It does not need an advance warning. It will, it is believed, respond to any challenge. But such a response, necessary though it may be, marks a failure of theory. The theory is that anything or anyone, knowing that the Deterrent is waiting, will not come.

The Deterrent is still being improved. Breeders are working on two strains. One is the Credible Deterrent, about which there is a small measure of doubt: Will it really deter? Or merely defend? This type of Deterrent has been developed from the American Bison, whose strength is in its passive stand.

The other is the Incredible Deterrent. Which is what the Credible Deterrent sees when looking into a mirror.

THE DILEMMA

Three principal types of Lemmas have been identified. The Dilemma, or two-horned Lemma, is most common. The Trilemma, quite rare, is believed to reflect a recessive gene of the now extinct unicorn, which once must have broken its rule of celibacy to mate with a Dilemma. In a third class is the Hornless Lemma, either Polled or Dehorned.

The Common Dilemma is a distracted animal. Usually its right eye is directed at the tip of its right horn and its left eye at the tip of its left horn.

The horns of the Dilemma are particularly favored as trophies by debaters. A good debater usually has a rack or two of Dilemma horns mounted in his study as evidence of his victories over the subjects impaled thereon.

Lemmas sometimes are found, but more often they are faced or confronted. In such a situation, salvation lies in the Viable Alternative, but in this fix, the Viable Alternative tends to get quickly impaled and ground under foot.

DRIVING COWS & DRIVING PIGS

Every President, possibly every politician, should know the basic difference in the technique of driving cattle and that of driving hogs. In the case of cattle, the herd should be started slowly and quietly. Cattle should not be alarmed or startled. When stirring a herd to movement, cowboys sing "Get along little doggies," or similar songs. Once a herd is started the speed of its movement should be gradually accelerated until, as the cattle approach the loading pens, the drive becomes almost a stampede, allowing the cattle little time or space for reconsideration of their course.

President Johnson's methodology was drawn directly from his experience in handling cattle. It worked on most issues he was advancing, until its final application to the war in Vietnam, an issue which required, if it was to be carried out successfully, the use of hog psychology and methodology.

The method for driving hogs is quite the opposite of that to be used on cattle. To start pigs it is necessary to panic them. Hog-drovers beat on pens and pig troughs. They shout at pigs in Latin, crying, "Sui, sui…" Once pigs are started the pace should be slowed down very subtly, so that the pigs arrive at the desired point just as they are about to come to a halt. If pigs are moved in this way, they will usually walk right into the pen or loading chute as though they had discovered it.

The greatest mistake that can be made in driving hogs is to start them fast; then allow them to slow down; and then try to accelerate the drive. The attempted speed-up can end only in disaster. Pigs go off in every direction and even turn around and come back through the legs of the drovers. In a large field, it may take days to reassemble the herd, quiet it down and prepare it for the next panicked start.

As a rule, the hog technique is better for dealing with the Senate on complicated issues and the cow technique is for handling the House of Representatives. President Carter was inclined to use the pig psychology on most issues, with little success.

THERE'S DWARFISM IN HIS FAMILY

An expression used at least once by President Johnson to mark a politician in whom he lacked confidence. The statement was incomprehensible to reporters hearing it for the first time, until it was explained to them that it was an expression wholly comprehensible to persons who raised Hereford cattle. President Johnson raised Hereford. Inbreeding of Hereford will sometimes lead to their having dwarf calves, sure evidence of bad genes and an occurrence disqualifying the line for further breeding.

EEE

The Emerging Equation

Equations are aquatic animals. They feed on key factors, which are rather like plankton in political seas, and often they remain submerged for long periods of time. Indeed, Equations may remain undiscovered for decades or more, while Equation hunters, in the fashion of whalers, search them out. Like Captain Ahab, they are always looking for the right Equation.

It is believed by Equation hunters that if only the right Equation can be found, many good things will follow. There will be peace and justice. The lion will lie down with the lamb.

Columnist Joseph Kraft is one of the great Equation hunters of our time, especially for the Middle East Equation - which is very hard to find. Some Equation experts say that it is in the Persian Gulf; others say it is in the Red Sea or the Gulf of Aqaba, or in the Gulf of Aden, or even in the Suez Canal. Some students of early Equation history say that in fact it is submerged in the Dead Sea. Others say it moved to the Indian Ocean last August.

The search for the right Equation in the Middle East has been going on for roughly four thousand years. Occasionally diplomats have thought that the right Equation had been found, only to have it submerge. Several times an Equation, believed to be the right one, has been found beached on page one of The New York Times, only to have it turn out to be the wrong one after all.

Some cynics say that the search for a Middle Eastern Equation is futile, that it does not in fact exist. But hi, ho, and never say die. Even Walter Cronkite, a skeptical fellow, has expressed cautious optimism that the right Equation one day will be found in the Middle East. Since this significant expression of hope, Mr. Kraft and other Equation hunters have again taken to sea and have tentatively suggested that they have seen an Emerging Equation somewhere in the vasty deeps between Tel Aviv and Cairo.

FFF

THE FILIBUSTER & THE DILATORY MOTION

The Senate wing of the U.S. Capitol ordinarily is thought about, when it is thought about at all, only in terms of the Senate chamber, the adjoining lobbies, the Vice President's office, and the visitors' galleries on the floor above. Not much is written or said of the dozens of little nooks and crannies and private offices where Senators go when they want to hide from their constituents or from other Senators. In one of these snug cubbyholes dwells the Filibuster, a beast whose talent is not to terrify but to bore. Sharing quarters with the Filibuster is his friend and constant companion, the Dilatory Motion.

The two of them seldom appear on the Senate floor. Often months will go by while the Filibuster and the Dilatory Motion snooze in their comfortable quarters. They eat old Congressional Records; they read books that are both long and dull; sometimes they memorize bum poetry, famous orations, biblical quotations, and recipes for Southern gumbo.

But the day comes when suddenly they are summoned to action by the cry of a quorum call. Blinking his innocent eyes, the Dilatory Motion ambles to the floor and offers himself, with a litter of amendments, freely to be disposed of. At the end of a busy legislative day, the Dilatory Motion often is found upon the table.

Meanwhile, the Filibuster curls complacently at the feet of the Senators who have summoned his aid. His purpose is to get inoffensively in the way of all pending business.

Now and then the torpor is interrupted by spurts of activity. The Majority Leader sounds a blast upon his horn. Cloture! Then our drowsy subjects take to their heels with the agility of foxes pursued by hunters. But such activity rarely is observed. The normal patter is for the pursuit to be called off and for the Filibuster and his furry companion to waddle back to their lair. There they hibernate, renewing their strength while they wait to be summoned anew.

GGG

THE RUNNING GAMUT

Running the Gamut is thought to be an ancient pastime, not unlike the running of hares or of foxes, or even of possums and raccoons. Musicians were the first to run the Gamut, but they were followed quickly by actors, by politicians, and by sawdust preachers at Southern revivals.

It will be seen, however, that Gamuts differ from foxes, raccoons, and rabbits. These familiar creatures like to run and will run on their own, sometimes just for the fun of running. On the other hand, they do not like to be chased. At least it is not clear that they do.

Gamuts, on the contrary, will not run on their own. They have to be run, or chased. It is their function and their delight. Often Gamuts are run with little direction and purpose. Sometimes they are run like pointers and setters, quartering a field, through briars and brush. Sometimes they are run between two points. Dorothy Parker is supposed to have harpooned an actress who "ran the Gamut of emotions from A to B." In January 1978, President Carter in his State of the Union Message ran the Gamut of proposed Reforms from airline regulation to public welfare. That particular Gamut leaped over eighteen Reforms. It proved to be sixteen Reforms too many.

THE FLEXIBLE GOAL

The Flexible Goal was first identified by Joseph A. Califano, Jr., Secretary of Health, Education and Welfare, in the early spring of 1977. He was striding along the banks of the Potomac, deep in thought, pondering the distribution of Federal aid for higher education. Already acclaimed as a man of action, Mr. Califano wanted to be still better known as a man of affirmative action, but the path to that reputation was filled with potential pitfalls. His task was to fix certain numerical quotas without actually fixing the quotas numerically: a tough assignment. Then suddenly he spied in the grass beside the river a friendly reptile, comfortably curled against a weeping willow. It was the Flexible Goal, a shapely and sinuous creature, dressed in jade green and carrying an abacus. Mr. Califano peered into the creature's melting eyes and saw that his problems were solved. For the Flexible Goal was his heart's desire.

This Goal is not a Goal, exactly. Neither is it a quota, precisely. The Flexible Goal feeds on specific percentages but it never gives birth to numbers, absolutely. A mature Flexible Goal asks only to be pursued in good faith; it is not to be captured, this year or next; it is only to be sought after or aspired to. For the bureaucratic sportsman who abhors quotas, the Flexible Goal makes the perfect companion. It is capable of coiling, uncoiling, sliding, slipping, amending, revising, perpetually nearing - it defies definition. In the world of affirmative action (Mr. Califano's world), it is the symbol of rubbery rigidity, the sign of positive vagueness.

FAINTING GOATS

The Bush Administration, more than any other recent administration, including that of President Clinton, which is beginning to show signs that it suffered from the same disability, demonstrated behavior characteristic of a breed of Oriental goats, known as the "fainting goats." These goats, which according to television reports, are now being bred in the United States, are distinguished by one particular behavioral act. At the approach of trouble they experience a sudden muscular seizure. Their eyes become fixed, their bodies

rigid. They fall to the ground in what appears to be a dead faint, a condition approaching rigor mortis. After the danger, the challenge, or conflict of interest passes, they recover.

In the Bush Administration, Assistant Secretary of State nominee, Lawrence Eagleburger, because of possible confusion of his previous interest when he was out of government, reported that he would recuse himself in any case involving countries, possibly even continents, in which he had an interest. There was no report of his having recused himself on any matter coming to his attention in office.

The Bush nominee to be Secretary of Commerce, Robert Mosbacher, announced that he would not be involved in decisions dealing with gas and oil or cosmetics. Oil he would avoid because of his own interests, and cosmetics because his wife at that time was head of a cosmetic company whose special trade secret was, and is, I assume, something found in the placenta of sheep.

The Bush nominee to be Secretary of Veterans Affairs promised that he would recuse himself, or faint away, at the approach of any matter involving the Veterans Administration and a Chicago funeral home in which his wife, Bonita (also known as J.J. Hickey), a registered mortician in Illinois, did business.

If the process of recusing is continued, it may be necessary to appoint two or three persons to each cabinet position so that at all times at least one may be ready and free to act without fainting or ethical compromise. Department business could be conducted in the manner of tag-team wrestling, with one or two substitutes standing ready to leap into the ring if the acting secretary falters upon reaching a zone of conflict of interest.

The concluding demonstration of the fainting goat syndrome occurred in the ending of the pursuit of Sadaam Hussein at the point of victory. The Clinton Administration suffered from the fainting-goat syndrome, most notably in the selection of an Attorney General, its early stimulus package, and in continuing concessions to opposition to its tax and debt reduction policies and programs.

THE GOBBLEDEGOOK

Of all the creatures catalogued in this Bestiary, none is more familiar, none more widely distributed in North American, than the Gobbledegook.

This lamentable beast has some of the characteristics of the common garden toad: He sits there, stolidly blinking, warts and all. He has some

of the characteristics of the pole cat and inky squid, whose properties are to spread a foul diffusion. He has the gaudy tail of a peacock, the impenetrable hide of the armadillo, the windy inflatability of the blowfish.

It is commonly thought that the Gobbledegook resides only at seats of government, chiefly at the seat of national government, but this is not true. The Gobbledegook is equally at home in academic groves and in corporate mazes. He is often observed on military reservations, in doctors' offices, and in judicial chambers. He feeds on polysyllables, dangling participles, and ambivalent antecedents. He sleeps in subordinate clauses. The Gobbledegook is composed mostly of fatty tissues, watery mucus, and pale yellow blubber. The creature is practically boneless. Owing to cloudy vision, once he has launched into a sentence, he cannot see his way clear to the end.

In the foggy world of the Gobbledegook, a janitor becomes a material waste disposal engineer and a school bus in Texas a motorized attendance module. Here meaningful events impact; when they do not impact, they interact; sometimes they interface horizontally in structural implementation.

For all its clumsiness, the Gobbledegook is amazingly adept at avoiding capture. President Carter pursued his quarry through ten thousand pages of the Federal Register and emerged with no more than a couple of tail feathers plucked on the trail. The beast can survive for months on a jar of library past; when startled by an angry editor, the Gobbledegook fakes a retreat, spouting syntactical effluvium as it goes, but once the editor's back is turned, the beast appears anew. It cannot be killed; it cannot even be gravely wounded. It dwells in thickets, in swamps, in heavy brush, in polluted waters, in the miasmic mists of intentional obfuscation.

HHH

THE HINNY & THE MULE

The Mule, as animal breeders and most politicians know, is the product of the crossing of a Jackass and mare. The offspring is sterile, but although sometimes stubborn and vicious, is a useful, hard-working animal. It is the term applied to Republicans who become Democrats, a kind of hybrid, for example Senator Wayne Morse.

The Hinny, on the other hand, is what is born of the crossing of a stallion and a she-ass. The result is discouraging and generally not useful. In politics the hinny is equivalent to what results when a Democrat becomes a Republican, according to non-hybrid Democrats.

Hunting in Pairs

I am indebted to Frank Paskewitz a local and state politician in Minnesota in the 1940s who observed of two of his political opponents that they were like cheetahs, in that they, as Frank said, "hunted in pairs." I have not checked or attempted to verify with naturalists whether cheetahs do in fact hunt in pairs, but certainly there is evidence of husbands and wives, in politics, hunting in pairs. The most notable literary example is probably that of Macbeth and Lady Macbeth.

In recent United States political history there have been several examples, none approaching the Macbeths, but identifiable. George Romney and his wife were vicious but they were a formidable pair. In the Johnson Administration Walt Rostow and his wife, Elspeth, were a formidable couple. Dan and Marylyn Quale would certainly fall within the range of the Paskewitz generalization, and possible President Clinton and Hillary Rodham.

A defensive refrain was composed in Minnesota to this end:

"He held the lantern
while Maybel chopped the wood.
He held the lantern as any
good man should."

III

THE IMPASSE

Although Impasses are found on all continents, the most serious Impasse, the most impassive, is to be found in the desert areas of Northern Africa and in the arid regions of the Middle East. For some reason not yet determined, Impasses appear to be moving out of their normal range.

At Helsinki in July 1975, experts thought they saw an Impasse near the hotel where the Americans were staying. It turned out to be only a cold moose. A second report of an Impasse in Damascus in 1977 was discounted when the Impasse disappeared before its presence could be confirmed by independent observers. Newsweek in April 1978 reported a fully verified Impasse in Bagdad. It hung around until summer.

Not much can be done to drive off an Impasse. Usually it will hold its position until the interloper who has come upon it goes away.

The best rule for dealing with Impasses is to avoid them or to circumvent them. In the case of the Bagdad Impasse, investigators found that there was no scarcity of food in the normal range of the Impasse. It is assumed that the Impasse came down to the city to get away from a stale mate in the desert.

The Untouchable Incumbent

Incumbents were not always as untouchable as they are now. There was a time when Non-Incumbents were quite free to challenge Incumbents, to touch them, to wrestle with them, even (as it is said) to unseat them. But gradually Incumbents began to develop special protection. They evolved in the manner of the porcupine: They grew longer and longer quills. At the same time they passed laws limiting the length and sharpness of the quills of Non-Incumbents. This was known as election reform.

Incumbents developed the special protective idea of seniority. This marvelous principle asserts that the longer one holds a position, the stronger one's claim is to it. Thus the Untouchable Incumbent asserted his right to certain trees, those with the sweetest bark and the most advantageous limbs for climbing, leaving Non-Incumbents vulnerable to easy attack down below.

Today the Incumbents feed on the juiciest leaves high on the tree, their diet consisting principally of choice prerogatives, traditional perquisites, special privileges, and fringe benefits.

On such a rich diet, with their tree-parking places carefully reserved, Incumbents tend to build up heavy layers of fat just below their quill-protected skin. This comforting blubber is called a pension. It is this on which they live, in the event that they give up their Incumbency, or if because of carelessness or overweight they are dislodged or fall out of their trees. In this case a new Incumbent speedily picks up the ways of the old, enjoys the advantages of Incumbency, and usually finds in those advantages virtues that he had altogether failed to note before becoming an Incumbent himself.

THE ECONOMIC INDICATOR

Economic Indicators are much like the groundhog in function, excepting that they forecast economic trends and conditions rather than weather. Also, Economic Indicators appear to prophesy on the first of every month, whereas groundhogs appear only once a year, on February 2.

The Indicators are wards of the Federal Government. They are carefully guarded by the Joint Economic Committee of the House and of the Senate, which in turn is helped in its care and feeding of the Indicators by the President's Council of Economic Advisors. They are maintained much as were the sacred birds of the temple in ancient Greece, insulated from corrupting outside forces.

In all there are about forty-five Indicators housed in the official compound. Twenty of these are Major Indicators; the others are Minor Indicators or Supplemental Indicators. Among the Supplemental Indicators is the Deflator Indicator.

In their underground burrows the Indicators feed on root statistics and give voluminous reports. They also eat developing trends. Indicators regularly give birth to Indices.

As the first day of the month approaches, the economic augurs, auspices, and haruspices gather to watch for the Indicators to appear. Among the famous augurs, auspices, and haruspices are Walter Heller, Milton Friedman, and Paul Samuelson.

Because some Indicators are treacherous and uncertain, and because some of them may not have fully digested their statistics or eaten their trends, expert analysis and interpretation are required. Moreover, because many Indicators are sensitive to weather, refusing in some cases to come out in the cold, interpretations must be seasonally adjusted.

INFLATION

Knowledgeable observers have positively identified only a few species of this unloved but indestructible creature. Two are Creeping Inflation and Galloping Inflation. Nothing has been found in between. Inflation never has been known to walk, or trot, or canter. When it gallops uphill in circles, it is known as Spiraling Inflation.

Usually Inflation creeps in its early, somewhat secret life. Sometimes an Inflation will creep throughout its life, but this is thought to be rare. Other times an Inflation will break into a gallop almost at the moment of its birth. It races across the country, leaping Indices as it goes. Its double-digit track cannot be mistaken for anything else.

Inflations usually are associated with the higher economic cultures, where both the creeping and the galloping varieties may be seen. In the process of moving a simple and backward country toward a more sophisticated economic state, Galloping Inflation appears almost an act of nature.

Inflation feeds largely on Staggering Deficits and Inconstant Dollars. After a full meal, Galloping Inflation can become Runaway Inflation. DO NOT FEED THIS ANIMAL!

[Left: inflatium gallopius fleetus]

KKK

THE KANGAROO & U.S. FOREIGN POLICY

Foreign policy of recent administrations has been roughly comparable to the reproductive process of the red kangaroo. Pregnancy for the red kangaroo lasts for only 33 days, not a long time for preparation. The offspring at birth into the pouch weigh only about .8 grams and are not well developed. The newborn does not leave the pouch until 235 days have passed. When the young kangaroo known as a "joey," does leave the pouch, it can be said, according to naturalists to have been "born again" for it takes on a different kind of life.

It continues suckling for a period. However, during this period the nature of the mother's milk changes. It is peculiar to the kangaroo that it can secrete two different types of milk at the same time; one to serve the young at foot out of the pouch, which puts its head back into the pouch to suckle from its original teat, and a second type of milk for the joey in the pouch which is attached to another teat. Almost immediately following the entrance of the joey into the pouch the female is impregnated, but the impregnated ovum remains dormant and remains so while the joey is in the pouch. If the joey dies, the dormant impregnated ovum becomes active and within 30 days there is a fresh joey in the pouch. If birthing prospects are poor for some reason (drought, absence of food, for example), the fertilized ovum remains passive until conditions improve.

The young kangaroo, out of the pouch, may be abandoned in favor of the joey, or even of the dormant fertilized ovum (this is called adaptive foreign policy). Thus in the case of Vietnam policy under Secretary of State Dean Rusk, the Vietnam involvement was presented as the "young at foot," settlement of a civil war.

The young at foot was abandoned, or nearly so, in favor of the "joey" which was in the pouch, namely invasion from the North, and both of these subordinated to the impregnated ovum "the security of the free world."

The policy of the Carter Administration, with Cyrus Vance as Secretary of State, relative to Iran also conformed to the kangaroo reproductive process, with three policies in place at the same time; one to support the Shah and his followers, the "young at foot" policy; second, to support the take over group, the "joey"; and third to wait, by going with the dormant blastocyst.

The Bush Administration evidently had a three possibility foreign policy relative to Sadaam Hussein and Iraq, and it appears that the Clinton Administration may have a comparable kangaroo approach to Yugoslavia.

A Hard Keeper

A hard-keeper, is the term applied to a horse or a cow that requires a lot of food to keep it going and actively producing. If the animal requires too much food for what it produces it is customarily disposed of. In political application, a hard-keeper is one who requires a lot of money to stay in office or to be re-elected. Reports of what various candidates spend in their campaigns are an indicator of their keeping status.

LLL

UP TO THE LICK-LOG

The Texan and Western images, metaphors, of life on the range and of handling cattle lent themselves well to politics. President Johnson and other politicians from cattle country used their experience and knowledge of the language often in political exchanges.

"We're up to the lick-log now" is a meaning roughly comparable to "fish or cut bait" and was used to describe a situation in which a political confrontation took place, and one or the other of the contestants had to fight or give ground, as when two range bulls arrived at the lick-log (a hollowed-out log holding salt for range cattle) at the same time.

ABRAHAM LINCOLN, OF CUTTLEFISH & HOUND DOGS

Abraham Lincoln often used animal metaphors and analogies to score points against political opponents. In the Lincoln-Douglas debates he did not refer to Douglas as a Senator, but as a "toothless" lion, a frightened bear, and a "cuttlefish." This label might well have gotten Lincoln into trouble had Douglas been a frightening man. A cuttlefish is a squid-like mollusk having ten arms and secreting a dark inky fluid.

When Lincoln in political controversy with one James Shields, a Democratic office holder in Illinois and later a Senator from Minnesota, wrote that after involvement with Shields there was not much left, and that what was left, was like the light drifting fur remaining after a cat fight, Shields challenged Lincoln to a duel, which progressed beyond choice of weapons and of site, until wiser heads intervened.

This was a particular application, but Lincoln used animal comparisons for more general application, most notably in his long poem "The Bear Hunt." In the early stages of the hunt he singles out one dog as lagging behind the pack. But near the end of the hunt while the argument goes on as to which hound first drew blood, thereby establishing his owner's claim to the hide of the dead bear, Lincoln wrote of the late arrival of the same hound:

> *"With grinning teeth, and up-turned hair*
> *Brim full of spunk and wrath*
> *He growls and seizes on dead bear,*
> *And shakes for life and death."*

And ends the poem with a commentary on politicians:

> *"Conceited whelp! We laugh at thee*
> *Nor mind, that not a few*
> *Of Pompous, two-legged dogs there be*
> *Conceited quite as you."*

THE LOOPHOLE

The first thing to understand about the Loophole is that it exists for one reason only: to be slipped through. This is all that a Loophole does.

A Loophole has this in common with Beauty, with Justice, and with a Fair Contract: It exists only in the eye of the beholder. For many years the most famous and familiar Loophole was the Oil Depletion Allowance. Those who were opposed to this provision of the Tax Code had no doubts or reservations: This was an Indefensible Loophole. But those in the petroleum industry had another view entirely. They saw the provision as reasonable, prudent, and wise.

The same skewed and simultaneous vision obtains in the matter of three-martini luncheons, Country Club dues, the maintenance of yachts and private airplanes, and the losses declared on the raising of beef cattle. One Man's Loophole is another man's Sensible Clause.

The Loophole lives only within the subterranean shelters of the Tax Code. It swims in the dark waters of obscurity. Now and then it surfaces, gazes about with its bland and innocent eye, and then submerges before the random shots of the people who run Common Cause. The Loophole feeds exclusively, of course, upon the plankton of tax benefits. Its steel scales protect it from editorial attack. It lives almost forever. The Loophole is constantly assailed by poor demagogues and rich politicians but it seldom is destroyed. Properly domesticated, the Loophole makes a faithful and engaging pet. People who have their own Loopholes almost never let them go.

MMM

THE MANDATE

Mandates come in as many varieties as finches, warblers, sparrows, and Southern politicians. They are generally divided into Greater Mandates and Lesser Mandates.

Among the Greater Mandates are the Impressive Mandate and the Overwhelming Mandate. The Lesser Mandates include the Slim Mandate, the Doubtful Mandate, and the Uncertain Mandate.

Greater Mandates usually are discovered almost immediately after elections, gamboling about the White House lawn. They appear like tree frogs in early March or old friends after a victory at the polls.

Lesser Mandates are more difficult to find, even though they come in many sizes and forms. Highly sensitive presidents and other elected officeholders rarely perceive a Slim Mandate. Political columnists, however, regularly confirm valid sightings.

Some Mandates, of course, are more visible than others. And in certain circumstances, even a Greater Mandate may disappear altogether. In November 1972, it will be recalled, an Overwhelming Mandate was widely remarked. But by the early summer of 1974, this curious creature had become a Disappearing Mandate. By mid-August it was gone.

It is said by some students that a President of the United States, because of the special powers of his office, can create his own Mandate. The theory is groundless. Elected officials do not win a Mandate or achieve a Mandate, and they cannot possibly create a Mandate. The voters give them a Mandate or present them with a Mandate. These are the proper verbs. No other verbs may be accepted.

When a Mandate has been given, the Mandate must be acted upon. This is fine with the Mandate, for he knows he will not be acted upon for long. It needs only to be added that the Mandate has no homing instinct. Unless carefully watched and cared for, he will wander away and never return.

THE VANISHING MILIEU

No one has ever seen a Milieu from the front. Milieus are usually observed as passing or vanishing. The fault is not with the Milieu but with the Milieu watchers, who become so preoccupied with the Passing Milieus or with the Vanishing Milieu that they fail to see a Milieu approaching. By the time the Milieu is recognized it is too late to look at its front end. This is true of all kinds of Milieus - Economic Milieus, Cultural Milieus, romantic Milieus, and others.

There are two schools of thought about the frontal characteristics of the Milieu. One school holds that the Milieu is cold-blooded and carries its head low (so as not to be observed as it approaches), and the other says that the Milieu is warm-blooded and has a long neck that it carries high, so that it can see whether the previous Milieu is gone or is going.

THE GATHERING MOMENTUM

The Momentum, before it has gathered, is a loose-jointed beast. It is as flexible and disjointed as a snake.
Until it has gathered, a Momentum is hard to identify. It may look like a Power Vacuum or a Developing Trend.
Its spoor is often confused with the trail of an Emerging Consensus.

Momentius gatherupus Americanius

The practiced eye, however, can detect a Momentum the moment it begins to gather. Like the slow pulling together of the furry caterpillar on its way to becoming a butterfly, the gathering of a Momentum is more subtle than the slow coiling of the snake.

Momentums will not gather unless conditions of temperature, humidity, air quality, altitude, habitat, and even barometric pressure are exactly right. The prediction of when a Momentum will gather, and the measure of its strength after it has gathered, are acts of science that are mastered only by a few political columnists. They alone can divine when a Momentum has gained impetus. Without impetus, Momentums are said to be faltering.

Amateurs and inexperienced observers should not take chances around Momentums. Once gathered, a Momentum can be held in check only for a very short time. Unless its wishes are granted, it is likely to break loose, like a hurricane, a flood, or a boozy orator, and sweep away everything in its path. Now and then, to be sure, a promising Momentum wilts overnight. The trouble, we are told, is that it peaked too soon.

THE MUSK OXEN DEFENSE

The Musk Oxen (also American Bison under some circumstances) in order to defend itself when hard pressed, forms a circle, with head and horns forming an outer barrier, and rumps together and thus stands its ground. This according to observers has been the position of labor leaders, with few exceptions, in the United States since about 1960. During the 1992 Presidential campaign, with approximately 7 million workers unemployed, and with reports that the hours of over-time being worked would, if distributed among the unemployed have absorbed about three million of the unemployed, the Labor movement ran television advertisements, favoring the forty hour week, plus over-time, for those who had jobs. A far cry from the position of Sam Gompers, who at the beginning of this century stated as a principle of action, "That as long as one person is out of work, work should be distributed until that one person was employed."

OOO

THE OMBUDSMAN OR OMBUDS-PERSON

An employee of a newspaper assigned to writing regularly or irregularly a column or article evaluating the performance of the paper. These critiques are customarily printed in a column on the edge of the editorial page or on the Op-ed page or a page near the editorial page.

The Washington Post and some lesser papers have regularly assigned ombuds-persons. The New York Times proceeding on the assumption that it is in need of no such continuing surveillance has no established ombuds-person, but submits to an occasional evaluation as to its professional integrity, to comments in column or book, by James Reston. The Ombuds-person has been noted as functioning about as effectively as, in a twist on a proverb, a chicken would if placed in charge of the fox den.

ON OWLS & MACKEREL

Rougher than the Lincoln cuttlefish language and than that of modern politicians, was that of John Randolph of Virginia who lived from 1773 to 1833. Randolf said of a political opponent, Edward Livingston, whom he first described as intelligent and as possessing other virtues and graces, in these words:

"He shines and stinks
like rotten mackerel
by moonlight."

Dick Richards, Representative from Virginia, in a moment of frustration, in a debate with John Williams of Mississippi in the House of Representatives exclaimed, "John, you are like an old Mississippi swamp owl…the more light I turn on you, the blinder you get."

PPP

THE PARADOX, OR PAIR OF DOXES

Experts disagree on the correct spelling of these feline creatures. One school holds that it is proper to say or to write simply Paradox when one means a pair of Doxes. Another school says that Paradoxen should be preferred. The third, to which the authors of this work conform, uses the better-established Pair of Doxes.

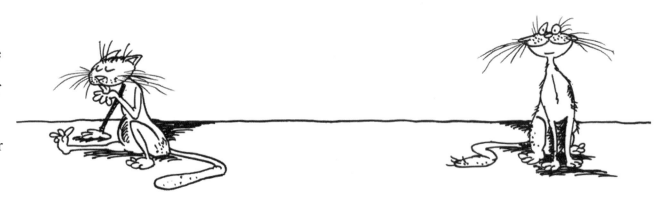

The common, or Ortho, Dox is never a threat by itself, nor is it disturbing. A Pair of Doxes is something else. Doxes always travel in pairs and threaten from two sides, unless they are old and have been around a long time, in which case they are merely distracting.

Unless a person has exceptional peripheral vision, it is very difficult to keep a Pair of Doxes within one's sight. They seem to have an instinct for staying just at the edge of one's range of vision. There they sit, licking their paws, heads tilted, as objects of skepticism, public comment, and awe.

The Paradox never has been successfully domesticated. A Pair of Doxes cannot be made to work together. They are forever raising their heads, asking questions, showing off. They go their own way. And because of their disposition to remain at a distance from each other, their mating is something of a mystery. Doxes frequently are seen in the same terrain with the Leaping Quantum, the Quandary, the Qualm, and the Dilemma.

THE PARAMETER

To persons of limited horizons - those lacking the world view of, say, the editors of Foreign Affairs Quarterly - a Parameter may look like a perimeter. It is not.

A perimeter is orderly and manageable. It eats only dimensions. Even a nearsighted person can recognize a perimeter and anticipate its moves. A perimeter will go around its subjects. It has no place else to go.

The Parameter is for experts only. Novices should observe it, if at all, only by telescope and from a safe distance.

The principal food of the Parameter is perimeters. A Parameter also eats grant programs, statutory authority, and regulatory limits. If hungry it will eat an anti-trust prosecution, a welfare plan, a farm bill, or a Trade Regulation Rule of the Federal Trade Commission. The tentacles of a fully developed Parameter will embrace urban policy, medical care, auto safety, and the marketing of edible fruits and nuts.

In the world of politics, Parameters live to be defined. Their arms embrace the illimitable and the unknowable, but usually they embrace the expendable. "Within the Parameters of our budget," people say. Then the Parameter, like the squid, emits an inky cloud and disappears. This is why it is so difficult to keep Parameters confined; they have a will of their own.

PEROT AND THE AARDVARK

The Ross Perot campaign continues as though there had been no election. He continues to make essentially the same charges he made before last year's election. His supporters seem to be just as enthusiastic and faithful. They rally like Amway salespersons. They are not a kook group. They are sincere and responsible citizens caught between the controlling forces of the two parties, and the ultimate winner-take-all rule imposed by most states in the choosing of presidential electors.

If the Perot movement were looking for a totem animal comparable to the Democrat's donkey and the Republican's elephant, it would have to be the aardvark. The aardvark according to naturalists did not evolve from any other animal or previous state of being, and it does not, and evidently will not, evolve into anything other than what it is. It is both species and genus. The aardvark, like the Perot movement, is a kind of existential experience, not continuing a politics of the past or moving to change or become something different in the future.

PIGEONS AND POLITICAL REFORM

Most Presidential candidates promise that if elected they will clean up the mess in Washington. The mess they refer to is never well identified or described but eventually at least a part of it is defined as that of the pigeons in the city, and especially one group of them, historically defined as the "Federal Flock", since they commonly range in the area of Washington known as the Federal Triangle.

Attention to the pigeons usually develops about mid-term of a President's first term in office or shortly before his second inauguration. President Bush did not have a publicly announced anti-pigeon program, nor has the Clinton Administration proposed a pigeon elimination or control plan.

The Nixon Administration initiated a massive program in anticipation of the inaugural parade after the 1972 election. It was to be chemically based, using a product, called "Roost-No-More" which, it was believed, would if smeared on trees along the inauguration route and eaten by the birds cause them to fly away. It was not satisfactory. Many birds ended up, or down, sick or dead. The Humane Society was disturbed.

The Carter Administration experimented with natural control, in trying to re-establish the peregrine falcon in the skies above the Federal Triangle. This effort, too, proved unsuccessful, as did a Reagan Administration attempt, consistent with Creationism, to drive pigeons and starlings away from the White House through strategic placement of stuffed snakes.

No one of these administrations seemed aware of the principle announced by Louis Neid the great pigeon controller of St. Paul, Minnesota, who advised people not to disturb and scatter pigeons, unless for a very good reason. Pigeons, if settled, on one building should be left there rather than scattered to others. Louis was opposed to taking politics out of the Post Office Department. It will show up in other Departments, he said, such as the Justice Department, where, like scattered pigeons, it can do more harm than it would have or was doing in the Post Office.

THE PREGNANT PAUSE

Until quite recently very little was known about the Pregnant Pause or the Pregnancy of Pauses. This lack of knowledge did not arise from lack of interest but from the difficulty of study.

First, the Pregnancy of Pauses was hard to identify. Second, the Pregnancy of Pauses was of such short duration that there was scarcely time for observation. Moreover, it seemed that most pausal pregnancies never went the full term, but almost immediately miscarried.

Students of Pregnant Pauses also were unable to distinguish between male Pauses and female Pauses and were therefore unable to study the mating habits of Pauses or to note the beginning of a pregnancy.

Much of the uncertainty about Pregnant Pauses has been cleared up as a result of the presidential debate of 1976 between then President Gerald Ford and Jimmy Carter. In the first debate of that campaign, students of the Pregnant Pause, together with some eighty million Americans, had the opportunity to observe a pausal pregnancy that lasted twenty-eight minutes. There has been no comparable pregnancy suspense since the world waited for Mrs. Dionne to bring forth the last of quintuplets in 1934.

As a result of the study of this longest-lasting pausal pregnancy, it is now known that there are neither male nor female Pauses but that the pregnancies are parthenogenic. It is also known that no matter how long the pregnancy of the Pause may last, nothing will be born of it.

THE PRESIDENTIAL HOP

The phenomenon that has marked most recent presidential terms has been an occasional overseas trip by an incumbent president, without clear definition of purpose or cause. The press and politicians of the party out of the executive power have usually been highly critical.

One of the most celebrated cases was a trip projected by President Carter in the fall of 1977. The President announced an itinerary covering four continents, and nine countries, all within eleven days. Had the trip been carried out it would have been an "historic first." The President had opened himself to criticism by having said earlier in his term that he would not leave the country until Congress had passed a satisfactory energy program. The majority leader of the Senate suggested postponement. Columnists and political commentators joined in the cry. Some said the trip was pointless. Some said that it covered too many countries. Some said that it did not include the right ones. Some said that the President should not travel and thereby save jet fuel.

President Kennedy after a trip to Germany for no particular high purpose of state observed that a president needing encouragement, or acclamation, or general crowd support, should go to Berlin. Sometimes perfunctory visits such as that of president Reagan's travels to meet Gorbachev in Iceland have surprisingly good results. President Clinton when he announced a possible meeting with Yeltsin in Canada was questioned and challenged both as to the time and place and purpose.

It is inexcusable for old Washington hands, in the press and in politics, to raise such objections. They should know that presidents may turn to travel out of loneliness, frustration, because they are unappreciated at home, or for other insignificant non-presidential reasons. But they should also know that there is a deeper, non-historical, non-rational drive. When a president is ready to travel he or she cannot and should not be deterred. That drive is best understood and explained in studies of the behavior of kangaroos as explained in a Scientific American magazine of August 1977. In that issue kangaroo behavior was reported and explained by three experts - T.J. Dawson of the University of New South Wales, C.R. Taylor of Harvard, and Knut Nielsen of the Duke University.

Kangaroos, these scholars note, do hop if they are frightened, seeking to escape danger, to find food, etc., but they also hop for the sake of hopping, or because they have nothing better to do, or to relieve and reduce buildups of kinetic energy, or possibly psychic energy buildups, kangaroo style. Presidents have similar drives, it seems.

PRESS BIRDS

The American Press (media) is (are) like black birds
on a telephone wire in the Fall.
When one flies away, all fly away.
When one returns, all return.
And here they are.

THE PRESS AND SELF-EXAMINATION

Thomas Babington Macaulay, 19th century English statesman, historian, and essayist, observed that there was nothing so ridiculous as the English people engaged in one of their periodic bouts of self-criticism, remorse, and moral reform.

Macaulay had never seen the American press, including the electronic media, engaged in a comparable exercise. Almost as predictable as the seasons of the year is a media bout in self-judgment and questioning during or following a presidential election. In recent campaigns the compelling concern, for a relatively short time, was that of whether the media had gone too far in inquiring, reporting, and commenting on moral faults and failings of candidates, their wives, and associates.

Following such examination, the media once turned to the case of NBC's doctored, and prepared, testing of the General Motors' pickup truck. On the basis of the record of the past there is little reason to believe that the press will beat itself into virtuous paralysis or reform. The end results are likely to be similar to those achieved when the monkeys at the zoo take to examining themselves and each other. The work is serious. There is much scratching of various parts of the anatomy and serious scrutiny of what is found. Sometimes what has been discovered is tasted. Sometimes it is eaten by the discoverer. Sometimes it is cast away or offered to another monkey, which examines the item, eats it, or casts it away. The monkeys finally appear to be deeply satisfied, reassured, and content. And life in the monkey farm goes on much as it was before the examination took place.

THE LAST PRIORITY

Priorities once existed in great numbers, sizes, and varieties. They ranged over great areas of the world. There were First Priorities, Rearranged Priorities, and Ordered Priorities. There were Pressing Priorities, Prior Priorities, Residual Priorities, and Last Year's Priorities.

Given such abundance, Priorities became a fad. Everyone had to have them as pets. Persons of high and low degree spent happy hours rearranging their Priorities. Because they are edible as food, tasting something like sweet and sour pork, in time they became scarce. Their fur was used as a mark of distinction. Gradually they moved toward extinction, like ostriches, passenger pigeons, buffalo and an honest martini.

Now only one Priority remains. This the Last Priority, identified once by President Carter. After it goes, there will be no more Priorities. Authorities are uncertain whether this last specimen will live longer if it is maintained in seclusion or if it is kept in a public place. Experts also question whether the Last Priority should be retired on half pay or used like a Low Priority until it dies.

Meanwhile, the Last Priority lives peacefully in a small corral near the White House Rose Garden, feeding on promises and asking only to be loved. President Carter, when resident, watched it every day.

THE GROSS DOMESTIC PRODUCT (NÉ GROSS NATIONAL PRODUCT)

Our Gross Domestic Product, in the eyes of other Gross Domestic Products, doubtless is beautiful. In a less prejudiced view, the Gross Domestic Product is not especially pleasant to look at. It is, to begin with, gross.

The GDP, as it is universally known, is a highly productive animal, and until recently it produced more than it consumed. Its equivalency measure, like the corn-hog ratio used in Iowa to compute the efficiency of pork production, was favorable.

In recent years, despite the efforts of fiscal veterinarians, the GDP has begun to consume more than it produces. Its handlers have had to import additional supplements, reflected in an unfavorable balance of trade and in Galloping Inflation. Its corn-hog ratio, as it were, no longer attracts admiration.

The Gross Domestic Product eats almost anything, from hog bellies to soybeans. Its favorite drink is oil, both foreign and domestic. Because of this mixed diet, its tissues vary greatly in strength and firmness. Some are in prime condition, taut and lean; others are wasted and flabby.

Politicians are constantly trying, like body builders through diet and exercise, to redistribute the weight of the Gross Domestic Product. They have had little luck. A few handlers, unable to turn flab into muscle, or to encourage or to entice the GDP to discipline itself, are advocating zero growth. This is no easy goal, because the whole metabolism of the animal in recent years has been conditioned to rapid if not to unlimited growth.

It now appears that, as with the dinosaurs, while the body grew large, the brain of the GDP remains small. Consequently its control over the body, especially the pedal extremities, has been less than fully efficient, to the point that some of the highly concentrated nerve centers are beginning to act independently of the central brain control. Experts are worried. What will happen, they ask themselves, when all the scattered nerve-cell centers become independent?

The hindquarters of the Gross Domestic Product may then seek to go in one direction while the front is struggling to go in another, and its disposition to consume more than it produces will get completely out of hand. This is what happened to the Gross Domestic Product in Germany in the period after World War II. It munched upon binoculars, 35-millimeter cameras, and Wagnerian sopranos, and it produced Volkswagens.

This should be a lesson to us all. Never give a GDP too much to eat. It may feed next upon you.

QQQ

THE QUALM

Qualms seldom are found alone. Usually they travel in a pack. Qualms are not aggressive but they sometimes are as difficult to drive off as they are to live with. They often appear when least expected and in surprising circumstances.

Whereas they are not threatening, they are disturbing. The presence of Qualms may discourage one from action or at least cause hesitation and provide an excuse for a delay.

Like Trepidations, Qualms will gather around the edge of a clearing or down at the far end of a bar. From such a distance, they cast accusing glances. Their eyes are large, dark, and unblinking. They give voice with a gentle, persistent bleat. Some people find the bleating of Qualms comforting; they regard their attraction for Qualms as a mark of character, in contrast to the professed serenity of persons who never have Qualms.

It has not been clearly determined why some persons have Qualms and others do not. Researchers are looking into the possibility that some physical quality may be responsible - as, for example, it is supposed that vegetarians never have lice, whereas meat-eaters, because of some physiological characteristic, sometimes have lice. Other scholars are investigating the hypothesis that Qualms may be explained in terms of some subtle relationship, such as that reported to occur on barges. Old bargemen say that in signing on a barge, a prudent deckhand will first look for cockroaches. If cockroaches are observed, the deckhand is advised to sign on, because - according to veteran rivermen - the present of roaches is assurance that there will be no bedbugs on board.

A few breeders, having caught a pair of Qualms, have raised them in captivity. A most successful group in attracting Qualms and raising them are the Liberal Republicans. Liberal Republicans like Qualms because they can overcome them. Regular Republicans cannot tolerate Qualms.

The Quandary

The Horn of Africa has attracted much attention in recent years. It has become the object of the study and reflection of experts of all kinds. Students of ethnic origins are studying it; African scholars and world thinkers have noted it. There is speculation that in many ways what goes on in the Horn is related to what goes on in other parts of the world.

In the midst of this anthropological and political interest, one naturalist has noted a previously unobserved fact about the Horn. Although the flora and the fauna of the area have been quite thoroughly studied and catalogued, there have been no reports in the area of the presence of the Quandary. However, on March 11, 1978, the Washington Post reported that one had been identified - noting that there is a "Quandary in the Horn."

This is both surprising and disturbing. A Quandary, especially if it finds a mate and reproduces, could quickly upset the political and ecological balance of the area. Quandaries multiply rapidly. Their period of gestation is remarkably short.

The most interesting observation about the African Quandary, experts say, is that a linkage may be developing between the African and East European strains which may eventually produce a new breed called a Detente.

THE LEAPING QUANTUM

The Quantum first was identified in the fields of mathematics and physics, where its jumps were measurable and irregular. Later it migrated into the range of political science. Now it dwells almost entirely in the world of foreign affairs, where its jumping is not only compulsive but also highly erratic.

This is the remarkable thing about the Quantum: It only leaps. Or if you prefer, jumps. This is all a Quantum is known to do. He does nothing else. He has no time for anything else.

This too should be noted: The Leaping Quantum comes from nowhere. He goes nowhere in particular, at least in the present, though frequently we hear of a Quantum Leap into the future. The Leaping Quantum was observed in the People's Republic of China when Mr. Nixon made his famous visit to Peking. Then it was said that China had made a Quantum Leap into the Twentieth Century. The Quantum Leap similarly was recorded in Spain following the death of Generalissimo Franco. Quantums recently have appeared in some numbers in Africa. They sometimes bound backward, as in India. Ordinarily, however, the motion is forward, upward, outward, on to infinity.

When Quantums mate, they mate for life or two weeks, whichever is shorter. Because of their incessant bounding around, they make poor pets but they make excellent tight ends.

RRR

THE REFORM

The Reform comes in various guises. The most familiar include the Needed Reform, the Imperative Reform, and the Too Long Delayed Reform. In every guise, however, Reforms share this common fate - their lives will be short and their permanent effects will be few. Like the vipers described in ancient Bestiaries, Reforms and Reformers tend to be destroyed by their own progeny.

The Reform may be ostensibly respected, but is seldom truly loved. The Reform goes abroad like a parson who has just hit the Listerine jug, smelling faintly of piety and antisepsis. The Reform is diligent and persistent and almost always worse than the condition just Reformed.

Reforms may be found in widely varying terrains, from the humblest home to the most sophisticated corporation. Ordinarily, of course, they are encountered in governmental situations, where the power of law may be imposed in their behalf. Early in 1978, President Carter succeeded Ralph Nader as the most vigorous proponent of Reform in Washington.

In the usual course of events, Reforms are spawned by elections in which Reform candidates seek to displace the politicians in power. Mr. Dooley, the eminent Chicago bartender, knew all about this. "A rayformer," said Mr. Dooley, "thinks he was ilicted because he was a rayformer, whin th' truth iv th' matther is he was ilicted because no wan knew him."

As Mr. Dooley might also have observed, such election contests have a dual purpose. The first, as to the opposition, is to throw their rascals out. The second, closer to home, is to throw our rascals in.

THE GREAT REGURGITATORS

Various kinds of ants have developed highly specialized division of labor within the colony, but have not quite reached the level of the Marauder Ants, which have some ants that act as warriors, both in defensive and offensive actions; another group that tends to the nests, the eggs, and newly hatched; and another group that gathers food for the colony. These are not unusual divisions of labor in other colonies, or in human society, both primitive and modern. The Marauders have added a fourth, special functioning unit, the Masticators.

These ants accept the food brought in by the food gatherers. They then devote themselves to masticating the food; what they determine to be useless or harmful they excrete. The desirable, nourishing (one assumes) protein, they then regurgitate, to be eaten by the Fighting Ants, the Nest Tenders, and the Food Gatherers, who are evidently deemed to be too busy to stop their labors to masticate food themselves.

In our society this function has been taken over, not in the selection and presentation of bodily food, but in supplying information and knowledge to those in our society who are deemed to be too busy fighting or preparing to fight, producing goods and services, or tending to the nests and the young.

Television, especially the network news services, have become the Masticators. All day long they masticate the gathered news, refine it, excrete or cast aside what they consider not good for the busy workers of various kinds, and then towards evening regurgitate what they have selected as mental food for their waiting colonists, the principal regurgitators being Rather, Brokaw, and Jennings with support from public television's Jim Lehrer, and other lesser Masticators.

THE INVESTIGATIVE REPORTER

As a consequence of recent mutations, Reporters now appear to be fairly well standardized into three specialized breeds: Those that work primarily on scent, like foxhounds, are said to have a nose for news. Those that rely largely on sight, keeping their object in view, like greyhounds, are said to have an eye for news.

A lesser breed, nearsighted and with little or no olfactory power, depending chiefly upon its hearing, is said to have an ear for news. They often become gossip columnists.

Investigative Reporters combine special gifts of all three breeds. They have amazing sight, like that of a hawk in the daylight and that of an owl at night. At incredible distances they can spot a smoking pistol, a dumb blonde, or a fat movie contract.

Their sense of smell is more sensitive than that of a truffle pig. The Investigative Reporter knows a truffle anywhere. He smells truffles from afar, in the same way that he can smell a publisher's advance.

The Investigative Reporter has a sense of hearing more subtle than that of the iguanas, the desert wasps, or the lizards of the Transkei. The true Investigative Reporter should be judged by his or her fidelity to the pattern of the Dung Beetle, his entomological model. The Dung Beetle follows cows. Some authorities believe it even anticipates droppings. Seizing upon the cowflop with its powerful pincers, the Dung Beetle rolls up small balls of dung and transports them to a hole the beetle has dug in the ground.

The beetle places the balls into the hole, then lays eggs on the balls. The eggs hatch and the larvae feed on the dung balls. The lesson of this entomological phenomenon should not be lost upon the perceptive reader: You can get a lot of mileage from cowflop, if you try.

REPUBLICANS AND THE REINDEER

Republicans are commonly represented by their totem animal which has little to recommend it for this symbolic role, other than that by report it never forgets, and in transit a following elephant will take its predecessor's tail in its trunk and follow. It has also been suggested that as some critics of Republicans say, the party is like the lower forms of plant and animal life, not very vital at the high point of its existence, but difficult, if not impossible to kill, like amoebae or paramecium, or like moss on a rock, slightly grey in the winter and slightly green in the summer. It should be represented by a mammal of lower order than the elephant, say a groundhog, such as the one found in Wisconsin several years ago in February with a body temperature of 38 degrees Fahrenheit and a pulse of ten beats to the minute.

A severe critic of recent Republican party activities has suggested the reindeer. By report, if in crossing a fjord, the leader of a reindeer gets turned about until he sights the rear of the last reindeer in the group he will follow that lead and the whole band will swim in a circle until all die. The Democrats are different.

The application of the analogy is challenged by the observation of the poet, Robert Lowell, that "Republicans are like the poor in Maine in that they cannot swim and will not sink."

SSS

THE MOST SERIOUS ONE

There are issues which are taken very seriously by those interested in them, and consequently advocated persistently year after year, with little success. One such issue has been that of anti-trust. Anti-trust subcommittees of the commerce committees or of the judiciary committees are among the best, or largest committees of both the House of Representative and the Senate. Each year the committee chairman or a spokesman for the committee or the sub-committee makes an appeal for more money or staff, informing the members of Congress that the concentration of economic power and control has become worse than it was the previous year, a report that has marked almost every year since the beginning of anti-trust legislation nearly one hundred years ago, and compares to the record of J. Edgar Hoover, who almost every year after he became head of the FBI would report that crime was worse than it had been in the previous year, and that he therefore needed more money for his agency.

The seriousness of these and similar efforts was fixed in the remark of Republican John Rankin as he watched and listened to the chairman of the anti-trust sub-committee of the House of Representatives making his annual appeal.
"There," said John, "is the chairman, just as serious as a pig urinating in the sand."

THE BUDGETARY SHORTFALL

Among all the species known to political ornithology, perhaps none is more familiar than the Budgetary Shortfall. This ubiquitous fellow nests wherever legislative bodies meet. You will find him in county courthouses, in city halls, in state capitals, and of course on Capitol Hill in Washington. Red-eyed, red-crowned, and red-breasted, the Budgetary Shortfall cannot be mistaken for anything else.

In Washington, Budgetary Shortfalls ordinarily are conceived in October, at the beginning of the Federal fiscal year. They emerge as fledglings just after the April 15 tax collections. By August they are full-grown, but they are peculiar in this regard: As they become fully fledged, their ability to fly diminishes.

The Shortfall may be identified by his peculiar cry, which is an off-key Uh-oh! Uh-oh! Uh-oh! It is the sound the Orkin man makes when he sees a termite. It is rather more pensive than the "uh-oh" voiced by South when the trumps break badly.

There are many Shortfall watchers, but in recent years the Assistant Secretary of the Treasury has ranked as the preeminent member and permanent chairman of the Society of the Budgetary Shortfall (SOBS). His function, on observing the decline in monthly receipts that presages the impending arrival, is to station himself at a window overlooking the east wing of the White House. When he is certain of his facts, he is required to fling open the window and to shout at the top of his lungs, "Mr. President! Mr. President! I have sighted a Shortfall! I have sighted a Shortfall!" then he closes the window. This is all the Assistant Secretary does.

Budgetary Shortfalls are not well regarded in the political community. Like starlings, grackles, pigeons, and cowbirds, they are publicly denounced. When Shortfalls appear in significant numbers budget directors are filled with chagrin. The Senate waxes wroth. Now and then appropriations have to be slashed.

Meanwhile the Shortfall goes on its awkward and embarrassing way, never running, always on the edge of flight but always falling short.

THE RELIABLE SOURCE

Reliable Sources sometimes are found within the criminal underground patrolled by officers of the law. In their more familiar coloration, however, they inhabit the fertile fields of journalism. Here they are quickly domesticated and become as tame as house pets; they require only an occasional feeding of flattery, plus the warm milk of public quotation.

Washington reporters have classified several breeds worthy of particular mention. Among these are the White House Spokesman, the White House Source, and the Senior State Department Official.

Reliable Sources seldom can be precisely described. This is because a truly Reliable Source seldom is seen at all. Often their existence can only be inferred from the tracks one perceives on page one in the morning. It is known that Reliable Sources generally inhabit shallow caves and shadowy places; they feed principally upon rumors fortified with a cup of classified facts; they speak from the side of one of their several mouths. They lurk.

Now and then what is thought to be a Reliable Source proves to be a Bum Tipster instead, but this sort of thing is rarely observed. Far more often, the Reliable Source proves to be completely accurate, for the Reliable Source is himself the source of the Reliable Source. During the delightful years of Henry Kissinger at State, senior reporters had no problem in analyzing the concerns of the Secretary; they talked with an Unimpeachable Source, and when the conversation with the Unimpeachable Source had ended, they said "Thank you, Henry" and departed.

THE POLITICAL SPECTRUM

The Political Spectrum is distinguished from other Spectrums in that its range of color is more limited and its shadings are less subtle. So far as the naked eye can determine, it begins on the left with ordinary barn red. In this coloration, the Spectrum is considered to be more dangerous than in its next color stage, a pink of two shades (old red and venerable pink) and one tint (parlor pinko).

In subsequent stages, on toward the right, color changes are accompanied by spasmodic body reactions called kneejerks. These were first identified by William White, one of the nation's greatest Political Spectrum watchers, in the 1950s.

The shades and tints of pink may be followed by a sick green range, usually identified with liberal Democrats. This delicate hue yields in turn to a blinking confusion. It is what the chameleon endures when he traverses a square yard of the Stewart tartan.

Here one finds a rapid change in political colorations of no commitment, from the baby blue of liberal Republicans to conservative grays and Old Navy blues, sometimes with a pin stripe running through them. At the far right we encounter the charcoal black reactionary.

Spectrum watchers who are interested in pursuing a serious study should consult the ratings maintained on the Congress by such organizations as the AFL-CIO, Americans for Democratic Action, and the American Conservative Union. You may then color the various members of Congress accordingly, from red to royal purple to black.

The Horned Steer

"Never put a horned steer in a feed lot, with a bunch of de-horns or polled steers. It will dominate the lot, hogging feed, and driving the others away from it. Grows fat while the rest fail to put on weight." This is a common saying among cattle feeders.

In politics it suggests the obvious possibility of domination of a campaign, a party, or a government, by the political equivalent to the horned steer.

The Syndrome

Syndromes are like mice and cockroaches. They are able to live in any environment habitable by man - below sea level or at high altitudes, in arid land or in moist and rainy areas, in cold or heat, on space ships or on New York City buses.

Some Syndromes are distinguished by moods: the Optimistic Syndrome and the Pessimistic Syndrome. Others are distinguished by the place in which they are found. Two Syndromes have been noted in the White House - the Oval Office Syndrome, which seems to survive changes of administration, and the Situation Room Syndrome, which President Carter brought with him from his submarine service.

Whereas the Oval Office Syndrome is reasonably quiet and unexcitable, the Situation Room Syndrome is noisy and hyperactive, although not as agitated as the Crisis Syndrome, which is not unknown to the White House.

The Syndrome is a relatively simple animal. If broken up it is likely to regenerate quickly into another Syndrome. Thus a quiet Oval Office Syndrome can become a Situation Room Syndrome, and even a Crisis Syndrome.

Both hard-shelled and soft-shelled Syndromes have been identified. These interesting crustaceans are like alligators: They have brains that are smaller than their cranial cavities. Thus, if a Syndrome becomes overbearing, the best thing to do is to flip it on its back, causing the brain to strike the top of the cranial cavity, knocking out the Syndrome. While the Syndrome is temporarily unconscious, the person being victimized by it can either escape or look for a friendlier Syndrome.

TTT

THE BLIND TRUST

Before the true Blind Trust was developed, scholars had classified several Trusts of limited vision, some with impaired sight, some that were one-eyed, and some that were indifferent to what was going on. All these creatures, whose common charge is to guard the dear old nest egg, were exploited to some extent.

Over the years a greater social need for nest-egg tending developed. The demand for half-blind and poor-seeing birds - birds that could be trusted with nest eggs - outran supply. Moreover, there was a suspicion that half-blind or indifferent Trust birds might show favoritism toward the nest eggs of birds who took up public-interest duties. Gradually the need arose for a fully Blind Trust. Once the need was recognized, the Blind Trust was quickly developed.

In appearance and method, the Blind Trust is a combination of penguin and chicken. Its large, webbed feet are equipped to protect the nest eggs until the parent bird, having fulfilled its public duties, returns to claim its nest eggs (or its young if the eggs have hatched).

It is popularly believed that the Blind Trust does not do much to advance the incubation process, but that it keeps the egg in just about the condition it was in when delivered. Some people doubt this. They also doubt that the Blind Trust always keeps the parent of the nest egg from seeing the egg during the period of trust. They suspect that the Blind Trust sometimes listens to the parent and takes advice from the parent as to the turning of the egg, the temperature at which it is to be maintained, or the possible exchange, scrambling, or poaching of eggs. There is also some suspicion that not all Blind Trusts are wholly blind, although they all wear dark glasses. A few skeptical scholars believe Blind Trusts can see in the dark.

Reform-minded egg watchers, led by Common Cause, recommend a Trust that is not only blind but also deaf.

WWW

WALL STREET: BIRDS, BUGS, FISH AND BEASTS

There was a time when the beasts of Wall Street were but two: The Bull and the Bear, both taken from the English sports of bull baiting and bear baiting, both carried on in an area known as "the pit." In old English prints the bull is shown as aggressive, charging the dogs in the pit, tossing them into the air, whereas the bear is backed up against the wall of the pit, in a defensive stance, warding off the dogs.

The bull and the bear still are the dominant characters in the market, but with the passage of time, and with changes in the financial markets, variety of securities, and of security dealers, many other animals, birds, bugs, and fish have come to represent participants and actions on and about Wall Street and other financial trading markets.

Some of the representations are rather simple and direct and have been in use for years. Among these are:

1.   Sheep, the innocent investors lead to the shearing shed to be shorn, or worse to the slaughter house.

2.   The Turkey: a bedraggled, stock or investment that is not performing well, possibly depressed, as the turkey must be on having been rejected, as the national bird, by Benjamin Franklin, in favor of the predatory, carnivorous, carrion eating bald eagle.

3.   Sitting duck: a company whose stock is under-valued: one with cash reserves, a vulnerable pension fund, over funded, or generally badly managed, and therefore a likely target for a take-over.

4.   Watered stock: a stock issued at a value considerably in excess of the value of the assets behind it: the term derived from the practice of giving cattle on the way to market considerable quantities of salt so that they will drink large amounts of water, thereby increasing their weight just before they are sold.

5.   Bulldog: a sterling denominated bond issued by a non-British firm or institution as for example; a bond denominated in sterling and issued in England by a U.S. based company.

6.   Gold Bug: an individual who thinks that investors should keep all, or a great part, of his or her assets in gold.

7.   A Panda: a new but obvious addition to the zoo, following the entrance, or re-entrance, of China into world markets - a gold coin minted by the Peoples' Republic, and exploiting or seeking to exploit what appears to be a universal, non-communist trust in the Panda.

8.   Shark: a firm or investor hostile to a firm's management and bent on taking over control.

A second category includes principally new securities, parts of other securities, and other market and marketing devices, that are represented, and made more understandable, if examined as metaphors from the non-human creature world. These included:

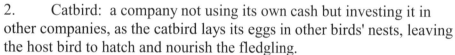

1.   The Alligator: an option spread on which the commissions are so large a part of any potential gain that the investor is almost certain to be eaten alive.

2.   Catbird: a company not using its own cash but investing it in other companies, as the catbird lays its eggs in other birds' nests, leaving the host bird to hatch and nourish the fledgling.

3.   Dehorned Steer: a corporation that has no active business and few or no assets (a kind of shell corporation).

4.   Boll-Weevil and Corn-Borer: inside traders, one destroys the cotton crop; the other corn.

5.   Red Herring: this term has been around for a long time. It is a prospectus that is given to a potential investor in a new security issue before the selling prices have been set and before the issuer's registration has been approved for accuracy and completeness by the S.E.C. derived from the smoked herring which was used to distract hunting dogs from accurately following a trail.

6.   Hinny: the offspring of a stallion and a she-ass - an asset that produces no income or capital gains; used to describe a loan on which the borrower is not making payments.

7.   Mule: a hybrid annuity in which a part of the investor's payments purchase units of variable annuity and the remaining purchase units of fixed annuity (more active and productive than a Hinny); offspring of a jackass and a mare.

8.   Possum: a company hiding assets and values so as not to be noted by potential takeover operators; comparable to protective immobility among rabbits.

9.   Swallow: a high flying, heavily traded stock that sells at a high price-earning ratio - marked by periods of rapidly rising prices, followed by a downward plunge.

10.   Church Mouse: dealer in securities and accounts of churches and religious organizations - security offering eternal salvation or temporal relief.

11.   Aardvark: a security which is not going anywhere and hasn't come from anything much. As the Aardvark, according to naturalists, has not evolved from anything and is not evolving into anything; a static investment, at most off-setting inflation.

12.   Elephant: an investment that takes a long time to gestate and produce any profits.

13.   Kangaroo: a triple option, comparable to the reproductive process of the kangaroo, which at any one time may have an offspring, out of the pouch, another in the pouch, and a third fertilized egg, in a static state, which becomes active if something happens to either or both of the other potential progeny, the one in the pouch and the one out of the pouch.

14.   Leg-lifting Dog: a practice of selling one part of a holding, while continuing to hold the remaining part, which may also be sold in small amounts.

15.   Dinosaur: an over-sized corporation (General Motors, IBM, for example) whose body has developed, while its brain remains small, or as in the case of some dinosaurs, develops a brain or control center near its tail section which sometimes gives directions not confirmed by the cranial brain.

16.   Dung Beetle: an operator that breaks up a large company into smaller components, and spreads these out hoping for returns from the dispersed units, as the dung beetle breaks up large concentration of cow, and other comparable, droppings, into small balls which it rolls away from the major deposit, places in a hole, and lays an egg on each ball. When the egg hatches, the larvae is nourished by the ball.

17.   Dogs: a general term applied to brokers and market operators, consistent with bull, bear, and pit, with bull dogs baiting the bulls, and bear hounds, the bears.

18.   Scorpions: of particular application to person or company, as the scorpion, while being carried across a stream by a turtle, announces, or acts with announcement, to sting its host unto death; in keeping with the nature of a scorpion "to sting."

There is a relatively new category of financial beasts known as "Felines." These acronyms, used by insiders and specialists used to identify packages based upon Zero based coupon treasuries and include:

19.   LIONS: Liquid Yield Option Notes

20.   CATS: Certificate of Accrual on Treasury Securities.

21.   TIGERS: Treasury Issues of various kinds.

22.   COUGARS: some variation on the use of Coupon rights.

23.   A non-feline of the same order, labeled a SPIDER, to indicate Standard and Poors Depository Receipts.

A last category includes various animals, insects, fish, birds, varying in intensity, magnitude of their targets, and methods, in their operations in the market:

1.   Lion: leaders in major takeovers, designed to kill the targeted object.

2.   Hyenas: individuals or companies that move in after the kill to scavenge on what the principal attacker leaves, to pick up spare parts or refuse.

3.   Jackals: lesser characteristics that circle the kill, hoping to pick up what the hyena leaves.

4.   Vultures: a pool of investors, waiting to purchase distressed or dying companies, especially those dealing in real estate.

5.   Piranhas: raiders different from vultures in that they do not limit themselves to real estate, but will attack almost anything, even before it is distressed or dead.

6.   Wolverines: companies or persons not bent on taking over another company but of fouling its traps and works, either for personal reasons or as making way for some other entity to take over.

7.   Killer Bee: an individual or organization that assists another firm in repelling a takeover attempt.

8.   Fainting Goat: an image derived from the behavior of an Oriental goat which, when faced by disturbing or unsettling conditions, falls into a dead faint, and remains in that condition until the panic-causing forces pass. In finance it represents the person or company which comes up to the point of making a takeover bid, or the financial institutions which seems ready to support such a bid, and then faints away.

9.   St. Bernard: the rescuer of a company, lost, or confused, in danger of death.

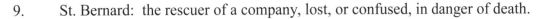

The Whelp that Laps Water

According to animal lore, a female wolf, after giving birth to a litter, takes the whelps to a watering place - lake, stream, or pond, and observes the drinking habit of each pup. Wolves, with real wolf character, according to ancient belief, do not lap water but suck it in in a kind of slurp. According to lore, if one pup in the litter laps water like a dog, the female kills it. Bitter Republicans used to say of liberal Republicans that they were wolf pups spared by their mothers even though they lapped water when first led to it.

INDEX

ABOUT THE AUTHOR & ARTIST

Eugene J. McCarthy is widely known for a political career that has included several Presidential challenges, but better known for his treatises on the metaphysics of baseball and figures of sport.

Chris Millis is a freelance illustrator who also does syndicated daily cartoons. A Mets fan who doesn't believe in The Designated Hitter he makes accurate renderings of irrational subjects from Saratoga Springs, New York where he lives with his wife Lisa, who occasionally finds him as sensible as he knows he is but funnier. His dog Jameson serves as his editorial advisor.